Origami Poems

and

Towering Stories

Poetry and flash fiction 2017

GW00701593

Earlyworks Press

Copyright information

ISBN 978-1-910841-44-0

Printed in the UK by
Catford Print

Published by Earlyworks Press
Creative Media Centre,
45 Robertson St, Hastings,
Sussex TN34 1HL

www.earlyworkspress.co.uk

Editor's Introduction

2017 was an extraordinary year for me, and for many other people –
in many cases for its unparalleled horror. This collection of poems
and flash fiction from the year includes memorials to the victims of
the Grenfell Tower disaster but also to victims of war, past and
present, and victims of lack of care, official or personal. It is not only
for authors and artists that one tragedy so often recalls another, and
leaves us questioning human history in its wonderful and terrible
entirety.

2017 was also a year of popular resurgence – of 'the many'
finding a voice in a year-long festival-display of different ways. The
works of art produced this year mixed the tragic, the angry, the
exuberant and the quietly pastoral. I would like to think that the
joyful and the tongue-in cheek take a legitimate place here alongside
sober reflections on tragedy, as a part of the memorial to those who
did not survive the year, a mourning for all we are losing to war and
strife – people, human and otherwise, landscapes, ways of life. This
collection though, is also a hearty cheer for those who survive and
will no doubt have more unexpected outbreaks of art and festivity
ready for the new year.

The one thing I really do not like about writing competitions is
that not every shortlisted work gets to be the winner, and often, more
than one deserves to be – but there is always subjectivity in arts-
based competitions, so please don't take a near miss to heart – in this
book we can read each other's work, and keep on learning and
growing.

Let us dedicate this anthology to the fallen, but also to the survivors,
to *their* memories, and to hope. Art survives. Write on. Read on.

Kay Green, autumn 2017

Contents

Poetry

Flash Fiction

How to Make a Chough: an Origami Poem

Begin quietly, and in the dark,
with a bird-base that has been hatched at sea.

Do not be scrupulous as the steersman,
or neglectful like the moon.

Lift a little light from the winter's mew and strand,
and take up the wide, pitch-paper.

First, make the midnight plume
by folding ink and slate across the horizon,

and then unfolding carefully back
to where the steel-blue raincloud lies.

Next, the wings in shining helmet-crankles
fit for kings, beside the still-beating heart.

Then press softly with thumb and forefinger
along the prickling air, whose flying-line may be

the whisper of a cleaving eye,
or the prow of a bloodied beak.

To make the skulking-cave,
take neap-lines from the draught-devouring tide

and crease them to the salt-cliff's foot.
Stand this beside the water's edge.

Display your bird.
Darkness drifts down in folded lines to the sea.

John Gallas

In the Forest of Khosrov

'a passing shadow does not mean eternal night' – Armenian proverb

The great oaks wallow. *Biff … boff … thud* –
acorns bomb the mud. Amidst the gloom,
hunched up in squeaking groins and trunks, a doom
of mother vultures phlegm their caustic cud
and rock, with hooded joy, their splitting eggs.
Something shades the sky. The mothers wind
their necks erect and shriek. *It swoops behind
the blown tops.* 'Hide your babies!' little legs
crackle at their shells. *It cuts the sky.*
Widow Airsteak strops her beak: the others
blink. *It scuds above.* The snarling mothers
crank their wings across their ogling fry.

A pink balloon re-fires above the hill
and drifts away. The woods lie hushed and still.

John Gallas

In the Gardens of the Baths of the Caliphate of Cordoba

Beneath the high hats of Sorrow
lie the long imagined gardens of Delight.

Here, writes Ibn Hatem,
the branches of the trees
entwine like lovers,
or,
alternatively,
if they stand
a little far apart
to be in a position of
convenient intercourse,
dance.

Turtle doves tuck up to sleep
like beating hearts
in the moonlight.

John Gallas

One of Three Ships

This place was affluent, the heart of tin, greatly prized
for its trade in bronze, and tales repeat like an antiphon

about a Tinner and a Lady on one of Three Ships
who sailed in on a frosty tide *(he did whistle and she*

did sing) with spice and gold and skulls
of old wise men. Legend says a child came too,

a sprig of a boy, thin as a thorn who, stepping merrily
onto the land, vanished into myth.

Today this beach is dismal, rocky and hollow
as a disused mine. A copper sun fades, our words

split up in the wind. The offing is dull as logic,
there are no fabulous ships to burnish our day.

I hope they played music for that Whistling Tinner
with a carillon of bells for the Lady, *for she did sing.*

Many Pannett

It was easier then, to write.
A seagull called on me at midnight

tapping its beak on window glass
with tips for a neat refrain

and Shelley came round
to show me some poems while Pliny

escaping from Vesuvius
shared his landscape with me.

In those days I relished
stars and moons and dawns

and sometimes minstrels
sang cadences of love.

Nature, in my verses then, was lavish
with falcons, skylarks, cicadas

and honey bees.
Even the fat grey worm dug in.

Now a sandstorm
clogs my head as men behind

a barbed-wire fence
die on their feet

and the realm of far away
becomes the setting for a sea of bad

where sinking children count
as less than sprats.   **Mandy Pannett**

Half deer, Half butterfly

Nagasaki 9th-10th August, 1945

My brother cheats at cards.
Shouts *koi-koi!* Though he promised
not to gamble.

He wins, always – the penalty –
drudgery. I do all the work, cook,
clean. Now he is hungry.
Too early for miso, that's for supper
when our father comes home.

We rummage for red-bean cakes.
Silent lightning shudders the walls.
We dive onto our tatami mats
cover eyes, ears, noses as the sky
falls in.

In the morning we look for father.
Mitsubishi has disappeared.

A gravedigger calls out, *Go home boys.*
Come back tomorrow, bring a jar, and tongs.

We pass floating corpses. *That boy has brought up his noodles!*
No, says my brother, *those are roundworms.*

Next day we return to the charnel field
with pail and pincers from the hearth.
His body is only half-burnt.

I want to run but my brother insists we take
home at least father's skull. He levers, but it crumbles,
brains slither out. We both run.

In the night shelter my brother spreads the pack.
Look, he says, *cards are mirrors, here is father,*
gentle as a butterfly, graceful as a forest deer.

Shoes moulded to his twisted feet.
Such small hooves.

Jocelyn Simms

Hovel

A greasy rivulet oozes beneath the lop-sided fridge
onto scarred lino. Syringes line the windowsill,
form a glass menagerie.

No one is here, save a moth trapped in sea-drift satin.
Taxi please! Flutters down the stairwell. My sister,
too precious for public transport.

Pictures torn from magazines, half-stuck to flaky walls.
Her clothes cling in a sodden bundle. Her bed unmade.
The minder's bed stripped bare.

An alarm clicks. We are under surveillance. Shakily we grab
a box of photographs, a keepsake or two. Step over the final
demand. Lock the door, pocket the key, hurry down the street
to the waiting car. Guilty as hell.

Jocelyn Simms

All the Names

A disarming country road, we imagine farmsteads,
a harvest stored, but where we'd assume church spires
splendid ghostly arches loom, as if

the Arc de Triomphe has replicated,
supplanting the cowshed, the corrugated
hangar, the falling barn.

No, not here, it's much bigger. That's Ireland,
There's Canada. Keep going or we'll miss the light –

It rises unmistakable: Thiepval's wall.
Slamming car doors we run, as if our lives
depend on it, up the track to embrace
the defiant gleaming sarcophagus.

You sit on a ledge, survey the symmetry of graves:
black and white, French, British. A chess board,
poised for replay.

The vast atrium lures me inwards. Thousands of names,
chiselled on white stone; grouped by regiment
or the battle where they fell.

I stretch out my arm, finger the gritty surface,
talking to the dead. I blink at the list, eyes
accustoming to the gloom. There engraved in sequence
lies my maiden name.

We fumble for the route. The bare arms of a tree launch
into the headlights as we ricochet along the bleak shoulder
of Vimy ridge.

At last, in Arras, we drop into a reassuring cocktail bar.
So, that was your Grandfather?
I shake my head. *He wasn't there.*
I raise my glass to the square, jubilant with Christmas.
But someone was, bearing my name.

Jocelyn Simms

Coffee Houses

Three hours from the sea,
Stamping out fog,
At King's Cross St Pancras.

We'd be in young, ration coats,
Out in the smogtropolis,
Away from our shy kitchens

Only knowing tea rooms,
Or the odd sachet of 'Chico'
At under-counter places.

In delicatessens, passed
By chokers of liverwurst;
London … a meaty city.

We bought the adult aromas,
Weird beans to make our
Apartment beverages,

In a block where fiddlers
Played on landings
Their odd Balkan melodies.

Lorna Liffen

Zones

It wasn't the stomach, taut, like cling film
over a small bowl of trifle,
or the legs, longer, thinner in
Pretty Polly hold-ups and wedge heel sandals.

It wasn't the waist, as clutchable
as on the first day they met,
or the breast buds, shaped
like hawthorn berries in springtime.

It wasn't the neck, with its swan-ness
apart from a few liver spots.

He said she looked pretty, lying down
though most do, lines melt away
into the sheets and pillows.

It was when she brought in cups of tea,
and trays of his favourite food
always untouched by her.
It was her hands
with the wrists of an alien,
with fingers like a ghost train ghoul's.
It was her hands
that made him leave.

Lorna Liffen

Barnett Newman's *Eve* 1950

A door sized slab of cadmium red, that's all
except for a lightly washed vertical
strip down the painting's extreme right hand side
in darker red a few centimetres wide.

An image freed from legend, myth or memory,
any kind of association, freed from imagery
even, beyond any painterly grammar,
perspective or compositional glamour.

That strip lends depth to the shining surface
inviting us into the endless red space
beside it, whilst in red contradiction
the flatness bars entry, infinity a fiction.

Spectators, we stand as though ignored
before the void. Alone and stranded. Awed.

Brian Charlton

13

No Plough Ever

(The Fall of Icarus, Pieter Breughel 1558)

The ploughman ploughs his furrows; they wind
around the field in narrow chocolate lanes.
The shepherd daydreams, grazing flock behind,
and on the sea the distant sun is in flames.

The fisherman leans, casts his line and thinks
of dinner, the fishy treat his children crave.
Unnoticed in the bay Icarus sinks,
his faithless feathers flutt'ring down in the waves.

It's not a question of cosmic censure
coming form a deity omnipotent,
says Breughel, but a comic misadventure
in a universe indifferent.

No clue here to any god's unfolding plan
and no plough ever stopped for a dying man.

Brian Charlton

Estate Birds

Rugged cracked concrete sighs
about the bleak,
the run down, deep
into the town centre where I wander
around aimlessly,
pecking at the Bin's rejected rubbish
with other charcoal pigeons.

The old broken clock face
clangs; we flap from early to mid-afternoon;
One hand gets bored of Two; a teen
Mother puts Baby in Buggy while we
welcome a wingbeat of peace in a solemn tune
within a punctured melody.

Our wings swipe their colour into clouds that hide
an autumn Sun, shining
decadently behind a silver screen,
not burning or blinding.
The fire here belongs on the leaves
That overhang branches like Youth's sweater sleeves,

and regular, flashing blue lights,
set to hunt some flaming thieves.
Concern passes like trains in the night.

Spiders sneak across symmetrical orbs of smashed glass
panes of a single-glazed window,
silent shoals of drifting litter and a crow
from the builder next-door,
who surveys crumbling bricks of old new-builds,
and listens to asses braying in the market.

A bowl – two bowls – a pound.
A thousand flowers
splayed on the ground.
I don't mean the flower stall.
Out here they live all for one and one for all;
brutal towers have brutal rules.

A hooded council,
with no currency to coin but the awry cry
of the unseen
estate birds;
we scatter as you hurry by.

Indigo Buckler

A Bit Bitter

And what about the gap-year verses?
Those, that are given graciously over Gatsby cocktails by the polo-shirt poets, privileged prosecco poetry penned by the people that perform in promenade at press nights and post-show piss-ups.

These guys; their Muse she was sleeping at home, whilst mine was sleeping around.

And what about the heart-broken, huh?
The brave and the bold and the blue faced boys who blew blue note into Bacchus stained brass in back street bars, whose spit and sawdust was their briar-roses.

These guys; their Muse she was sleeping at home, whilst mine was sleeping around

Then I met you.
Then I met you.

Danny Kent

Impressing Others

I borrow a pen – politely
from the Librarian.
She looks sideways at me
her outlook – Prophetic.
I retreat to the corner –
to *Write* – my intention.

My next poem will have Iron at its core.
My next poem will be a seething, living coloured mass.
My next poem will be carved in earnest underneath an arrogant
stone urn outside a cathedral somewhere in this city that once
thought itself complete but was not because it had not yet read my
NEXT POEM.
My next poem will have oak, gold, ink, elm, diesel smoke, courage,
travel cards, lager, cleverness, cedar wood and mint all burning
together in an odorous orgy of EVERYTHING.

Not this one.
I take the pen back to the Librarian and
I let my wallet wilt open.
I hope that she sees my poetry society membership card.

Danny Kent

Breaking up with the Kardashians

I lent you the Algerian
But you told me you did not understand.

Ts'anun Yem

You go back to watching Pine-coloured women tell each other
they are beautiful.

Chem Hakamum

Armenian Women.
A Murder of them.

Sirum em kez, Kartsun Yem

I lent you the Catalonian and Peruvian
I lent you the Californian and West-Londoner
I lent you no Middle-Eastern but still they came between us.

Fewer words were spoken that were understood.
Thank god I too was only borrowed.

Danny Kent

The London We Knew

Three-Tuns soaked and staggering
on One Portman Mews.
"Oh Marylebone, you're marvellous! Now home."

Half-a-pack-smoked and sitting
at Billingsgate Trafalgar Way.
"You know what don't get sold gets thrown away."

Steam-satin cloaked and caylpsoed
in Brockly Road's Rivoli.
"You've learnt a new step well gin first then show me."

> From Nine-Elms, The Gardens, The Strand and The Kew.
> Lovers of and Londoners, of which there's too few –
> – I'm sorry I'm just trying to hold onto this London we knew.

Danny Kent

The Old Tower

The tower, a staunch sentinel, still stands
as they excavate the inner chambers:
whispers intermingle with the embers.
The tillers pause, throw down their tools, demand
the end of reaping soil laced with salt and sand.
Lamentations rise like billowing vapour;
artisanal pride ebbs out of favour.
"But how can we plan for the unplanned?"
A Clerk of Works masked by shadows sighs,
wiping beads of sweat from his brow, the heat
singeing his cloak to his skin. The sky
suffocates below a charcoal sheet,
as smoke obscures even the brightest eyes,
and the tillers take scythes to their fields of wheat.

Matthew Adamo

I Have Seen it Happen Before

It happens everywhere, I have seen it before;
ghosts that haunt forest shadows left homeless,
follow the dark side of timber workers,
slip into cars that take the men home.
I have seen it happen before; streams of cyanide,
the other face of Janus flush with gold.
In a rainstorm stones wash down a razed slope,
crash into homes that stand in the way.
There is fire in the trees; witches in black
read coffee grounds and the bones of saints;
one day this whole area will be burnt to the ground.
Okeanus won't be able to stop the fire,
so close, even with his salt thick in the air,
ash falling on his silver skin.
It happens everywhere. I have seen it before.
People forced to flee from their homes,
fish dying, wolves without trees.
Forest workers return home; no forest to cut,
bare hills like sticks in a wild wind;
all that is left is the shadow of ghosts.

Ion Corcos

In Their Towers

They sleep so soundly in their beds,
Presuming safety in their towers,
And do just what the notice says –
They sleep so soundly in their beds.

Developers have made a wedge,
Contracted firms and misspent hours;
They sleep so soundly in their beds,
Presuming safety in their towers.

Sean Gibson

And Nobody There To Read It

Wrote what I wrote
In the dark,
In unnatural light,
Snatched hours;
Both hands to my brow,
Drilling deep to find secrets,
Heavy work, to fuel secrets –
So hard to tell
What's added, what's lost
In the process.

Did what I did
And what I didn't;
In this new light
The many cower.
Which shock would be worse –
That this could all have been real
Or that I could just dream this up, and steal
Your story so well?
What's added, what's lost;
Would you notice?

Sean Gibson

Nights Drawing In

Every few paces
Leaf scrapes under foot;
Husks
Everywhere you look.
No two the same, but
All of one tree;

The song of summer; rustle and sway,
The shock of colour on grey
Now fades.

Every few paces,
Leaves underfoot;
As mulch they are all
Much alike,
Rotting in plain sight.

We tread through devastation,
And all I care to mention?
I wish you'd pick your bloody feet up.

Sean Gibson

A Remembrance Found

Edgar Charles, my father,
inherited from uncles, gone before his birth.
Men unknown a generation later
only their names threaded through the years.
They did their bit in turbulent times.

And now, I hold a faded photo,
a picture of two proud young men in uniform
faces to match the names I know;
Edgar and Charles.

Elaine Beeby

Heron: Curry Moor

His leg the poised bow of a violin,
heron surveys the flooded Levels
then, with a cry like a wrong note,
he heaves into flight.

Sucked upwards by a white sky
where last night's moon
is sketched in ghostly outline
he banks and skims, wings billowing,
head beaked forward, searching
the shadow-washed water.

Turning again he contracts, folds himself
on to a half-submerged gatepost,
dark eye intent, concentration
embodied in a hunk of wind-ruffled feathers.
Essence of the Moor
in a hunched silhouette.

Sue Kauth

Where do all the birds go

When they die. Not eventually that is,
but at the exact check of death. Like now. Just now.
Expect you've recognised that dead
they're rarely seen. Nothing left on lawns even:
no beak, no claws, no feather-down, no bone.

But, yes, I know there are other places, other times.
Think roadkill – pheasants mainly –
zigzag-hassled and shattered in smudges of plumage
and runs of blood:
there's the odd brown job, too – sparrow, dunnock, wren –
cat-trophied home and left on doorsteps;
and crows hanging black-binliner-bags in rows
on fence wire,
but where, I ask you, do the rest go ...

No lying in state for the King of the birds – the convocation.
No session recess for the parliament of owls.
No sentence for the murder of rooks,
the unkindness of ravens, deceit of lapwings,
the scold of jays.

Nothing seen of the glaring of owls, their wisdom,
the congregation of plovers,
wake of buzzards,
the piteousness of doves.
Not to mention the exaltation of larks
as high as kites;
and as for the lamentation of swans – so heavy, so big –
no sign at all.

So where do the birds … Where do they go …

Like distant cousins in foreign parts, or spinster great aunts
who is at their committal, their internment …
Where is there any remembering …

Where do they all go …

Roger Elkin

Paeony

"The paeony resents being disturbed." – Richard Sudell,
       Practical Gardening and Food Production in Pictures (1906)

Finger the orb of her bud,
firm with the firmness of shotty glass –
smooth, round – its green and white
flecked with maroon
like specks of dried blood,
so hard, so cold
you'd be forgiven for thinking
she's done for,
well past her best.

Yet when days later she bursts into bloom,
flouncing fuller, fuller
like a big Mama in her best festival hat
she's such a blowsy dresser
that, sensing she's top-drawer,
she flaunts herself, clowning about
as if everything's gone to her head
and she's giving you the come-on.

It's then your fingers begin to linger
over her satin-thin skin
not that pink-silkiness of the newborn
not the virginal ermine white
but the red of the freshly-snecked wound –
shiny, certain –
as if sporting a warning.

Handle me, yes.

30

Finger. Stroke. Pluck.
Even cut me.

But don't ever think of moving me.

Don't.

Roger Elkin

Pear Blossom

Swollen buds at stem-tip
with skin-thin husks, baby-nail-shaped,
and hints of mint-green leaf,
furred beneath, tacky from sap
that lacquers our hands.

Urgent their burgeoning
in translucent whites, milk-bright
but tinged with pink stigmata,
their faces leaning towards light,
mouths agape in five-petalled keenings:
so many, so sudden.

And their scent, hanging over gardens:
a headiness invisibly-heavy
in a pall that summons fruitflies and bees
to knead stamen and anthers
with their Spring abandon.

Then a hush of release,
like an after-desire grasping,
and a wedding-confetti petal-fall
across orchard lawns
in premonitions of Autumn.

Roger Elkin

Teasels

Unputdownable
like North country vowels
so have been outlawed to corners
of fields, lay-bys and wasted-space.

See where leaves meet
in basal whorls that shoot upwards
tined with spiny bract and spur of spike
along their strap-like angled stems.

Snap one cracking open
to reveal its milk-white sap,
its insides of fine down
glistening silvery under sun.

Next, measure their Summer treasure
in confections of spherical inflorescence
parading jade to lavender-magenta:
aah, such delicate deception.

Come September, splendour
has gone to their heads:
Celtic-helmeted remnants,
almost barbarian in amber

and bronze, with phalanxes
of hooked tangs and brittle spikes
that match scratches with blood.
Theirs. Yours.

Hacked. Slashed. Cut down.
They're unstoppable.

Next Spring, watch their clans
lancing back over new ground.

Roger Elkin

Grow They Must

The Arran Pilot seed potatoes have been trying to grow
in the string bag on the shelf in Wilkinsons.

There's no rain and the light's not sunshine
but they put out shoots.

In their searching earth and the sky,
the shoots became long thin starving limbs.

At home it takes me an hour to disentangle each tuber
from the others and the string bag.

I put them onto a cardboard tray outside
ready to take to the allotment.

In the night there's late April heavy rain.
This morning the shoots have an idea of leaves.

Caroline M Davies

Arranging the Hours

At the gateway aconites
show yellow stars with ruffs,
then snowdrops glow
like dangling pearls.

Before first blossom buds uncurl
she gathers artless twigs
of catkin and pussy-willow.
Fanned in slim-nicked vases
they seem tip-dipped
in powdered silver and gold.

Bright strings of days slide by
unclasped.
But daffodils, narcissi,
tulips, lilacs pass
with pleasure through her hands
into old china and cut-glass
to recreate the masterpiece of time.

She bends to pluck
seed-studded strawberries,
jewel currents, parts
velvet raspberries form their jaded hearts.
Round the door twin roses twine.
He brings her soil-smeared vegetables.
As she rinses them they shine
like unearthed gems.

When Chinese lanterns hang
cabochons of fire on tinder stems,
with her cool touch
she sets them in a lyre-shaped urn.
The necklace of the years
encircles her.

At the gate primroses grow,
then dainty columbines
like trembling amethysts
shiver and blow.

Andria J Cooke

Rose Garden

Burgundy Ice, Iced Ginger, Peppermint Ice, Ice-cream,
Ginger Syllabub, Heather Honey, Hot Chocolate,
Crème de la Crème.

Fragrant Delight, Double Delight, Rumba, Candy Stripe,
Dairy Maid, Dainty Maid, Dusky Maiden, Amber Light,
Mermaid, Gypsy, Tawny Tiger, Amber Queen,
Anniversary, Valentine Heart, Waltz Time, Summer Dream;
Deep Secret, Osiria, Bridge of Sighs, Blue for You.

Big Purple, Moody Blue, Rhapsody in Blue, White Symphony,
Twice in a Blue Moon, Black Magic,
Nostagie.

Andria J Cooke

White Violets

No daffodils please.
Their brightness hurts my eyes.

Spare me primroses.
Their tenderness offends
my hardened heart.

Leave the bluebells where they drift
like misty streams beneath the trees
to take those braver than I by surprise.

Pick me no tulips
spangled with red and gold
too strident for the fuddled mind.

Bring me none of these,
for the shyest are over-bold.

Nor even violets.
I cannot bear their sweetness
too divine.

Unless it be the kind so rare who hide
in the deep dark hollows of the wood,
colourless and blind.

Andria J Cooke

The Cupboard

A slight man with a limp.
Shirt sleeves rolled up,
he bent to work the soil.
He'd come in from the garden,
plunge his hands in the enamel bowl.

His hair was scant,
his eyes loam brown
like the mud into which he was blown
on the killing-field at Ypres.

Once he talked and showed his scars,
exposed the shattered leg which grew no hair,
the hollowed upper arm;
safe in his fireside chair
reached deep into the murk beyond,
brought from the cupboard a souvenir
of the battleground.

In sepia photographs
he braced his crutches bravely.
They trained him into carpentry.
He drew a pension and raised a family,
then returned to view the cemeteries.

As he watered, hoed and dug,
perhaps he thanked that other earth.
The story was it saved his life;
covered him and stopped the flood.

Andria J Cooke

The First Frontier

A childhood sledge leads to the North Pole.
A jungle finds echoes in a garden overgrown.
A climbing-wall ends at the Old Man of Hoy.
Holiday sands encourage a desert convoy.
Little Jack learned seamanship in the bath.
So did his sister Jackie. And off they've cast.

Philip Burton

The Alwin Machine

A distant memory arrives re-touched.
The arcade machine, now easy to reach –

no tiptoes, no begging for coins – lurks
at eye-level, fresh clean as a fish hook.

Muscle memory thumbs the spring, hurls
the silver ball. Watch it cling and curl

down the retro solar system back flash.
Win game? Loss chute, the gnash

of milk teeth when the icon was lost.
Such rocketing fun. And made to last.

You gaze at a thumb, yours to control
interplanetary spheres permit you sole

rights to space-time. With a staunch
inner pride, you press, release, launch,

and – as when a child – each survival,
maybe five times, means you're a special

fooler of the penny rich arcade man.
He's welcome to the stained old cash.

Philip Burton

A Constable Moonlighting, Manchester 1911

I wake them up at the allotted hour,
this nightly supplement of mine, tapping
the windows of factory workers along my beat
of Alder Street to Victoria Avenue.

I test the limber strength of the bamboo cane,
reach the second floor windows, wait
for pale faces to acknowledge me with one hand
while the other rubs their eyes.

Agnes says I should be handing it over
to a younger man, take the weight
off my feet but I enjoy it.
I've never told her that.

It's like a magic wand, waking, summoning
these faint squares of light, dispersing
the dreams that we can't take hold
and the visions we want to forget –

– like Alfie Smith on a cowhide shield in Ulundi
blood spiralling out into the pattern, congealing
on the tassels while some Dutch doctor
tried to save him and me saying,

"pull yourself together."

I have a medal somewhere for that,
Victoria Regina Et Imperatrix, red,
purple, orange threads in a metal clasp
all I have left from the Zulu War.

I tried to talk about it with one new recruit;
He nodded and forgot at the same time.
Still he was eager and handy with a truncheon
when it was necessary or useful.

The red brick hives start to buzz as the men
step out, join the throng of factory speech,
I pass a lamplighter hoisting his pole, positioning
the hook to twist the tap that turn off the gas,

putting out the lights, one by one.

Glen Wilson

Old Dog Days

It's just too much – even for a catnap:
         folding up his spidery-thin black legs;

Legs which once belonged to a spirited
eye-catching young greyhound, but sadly now,
in these twilight years, seem more befitting
an angle-poise lamp than a prize-winning pooch.

One more push and he'd be in the final
         diagonal stretch of his comfy bed.

Instead, his soft black pointed ears, as slack
as wilting tulip petals, his two large
marble eyes rolling towards oblivion,
he's an old man, sitting with his back to
the sun, reflecting on the hares he should
  have snared, and the races he should have won.

AKS Shaw

Outside the Frame

(1914)

He smoked a lot, rolled his own, joked and cursed,
   cursed the mud, the food, the rats, oiled his gun
      a thousand times, wrote to mum, thought at first
         what fun to join his mates and trounce the Hun.

Like all of us he trembled, got the shits,
   but never faltered, walked out into Hell.
      There was no body, only fragments: bits:
         a scattering of fragments where he fell.

Yes, that's him in uniform: that photo
   on the sideboard, dusted ev'ry day. No,
      she wasn't told how he was killed – her son,
         her only child; remembers him instead
            as if the telegram had never come –
               the day he left: unshot, unhurt, undead.

AKS Shaw

Bushwhacker

In 2015 Australia posted its hottest end to any year as the impact of one
of the biggest El Ninos on record began to be felt across the continent.

Didgeridoo here he comes
hobbling out of the cobalt blue
out of the warp of hessian wilderness
this denim-laced ill-braced
curled up soul of a man – guy – bloke.
He's deaf as a prophet
in denial, prickly as old cacti
protesting that it's nothing but a joke
this so-called climate change.

The corks which hang from his hat
have popped their clogs long ago.
The dried-up river basin of his face
is still and brown as dead grass.
Eyes once as green as the horn of plenty
are like pips in the pit-holes of his skull.
Shielding them with the boomerang of his arm
he watches long fingers of bright sunlight
dissemble a necklace of thin white cloud.

The grass is parched
the trees are parched
the land abandoned
the river dry
reeds broken
billy-can brittle as dry bone.
Beyond him the road snakes away
into a rattle
of cracked stones.

He coughs, his throat scarred
by the crochets of an old folk song
which ricochet inside his head.
He spits a pellet of phlegm
into the hush of grit and dust
and hobbles back into the bush
still muttering under his breath
that it's the rest of the world, not him
who have got it all wrong.

AKS Shaw

For LW, Too Late

I knew a woman who when her belly swelled large
made jokes about the infant she was carrying.
Tight as a drum she visited her doctor who
smiled at her and nodded and sent her for tests.
Outwardly cheerful she kept her appointments,
long journeys made on dusty Green Line buses.
Though she winced and grimaced at every jolt,
she was obedient and grateful and hoped for the best.

That dazzling September through long afternoons
she reclined in an armchair by the window
where lazy emerald houseflies buzzed and
sometimes a breeze stirred her still dark hair.
Then with little fuss she lay down on her bed.
She was whiter than the linen she was wrapped in.
For a mouthful of milk she would lift her head;
a blackbird on a rose bush whistled her a prayer.

I knew a woman who went silent as a mountain.
Dusk spread its shadows and she seldom spoke at all.
Patiently she waited, her face turned to the window.
She never saw October's leaves fall.

Abigail Elizabeth Ottley

I have

Walked down a huge hall to face
Three giants with the Eleven Plus in their hands

let them write borderline case on my memory
with indelible pens

bitten my nails too short to scratch
hit my friend on the head with a biscuit tin

I have

discussed the symbolism of kettles
visited families night and day

seen toys bought on hire-purchase just for Christmas
to be taken back straight after

worked with warring psychiatrists – and a ward-sister
who claimed I was racist, then gave me flowers

I have

Taught truculent, tender teenagers
marked their work beyond midnight

felt gutted for a gifted pupil
penalised as a potential terrorist

witnessed a teacher white with drink
sick up in the staffroom, disappear to die

I have

been one of three sisters, Dad often away,
sick of female families, desperate for a boy

cried at the door when a gipsy selling violets
threatened I'd have a baby girl if I didn't buy

held my son like a porcelain doll, both of us breaking
tried to escape his screams by wandering the house

I have

watched my son withdraw from the world
into the darkness of his mind

fretted when my daughter left the family
searching for firmer ground

lived my husband's last illness with him
until the oxygen could do no more

bitten my nails less, moved on

Ruth Hanchett

Some effects of brilliance

1

From afar he beamed at his daughters,
gave them chocolate, loved them in his way.

Stories of his meteoric rise, child
from a council estate, dazzled them,

a shooting star in the earth's atmosphere
trying not to burn up.

Gold medals for medicine gleamed,
casting shadows.

He shed new light on the whole child
but only partly saw his own,

travelled through a galaxy of ideas
lighting up students with his lectures

yet asked a family friend on the stairs
Who are you? No small talk or no talk at all.

2

Whatever, whenever it was, she was ready;
wash day on Mondays, clanking the mangle,
shining silver on Tuesdays, no shadows left,
cooking everyday, breakfast, puddings, pies.

Hair moulded into waves, as in her perfect
wedding photos, she'd put away her career.
Boned corsets laced in her anger.
She could scold you scarlet: you're late.

She shone as the Professor's wife, moon
as to sun, until he dropped into his black hole.
Somewhere in the house were still hidden
medals she too had won for medicine.

3

Corners of the house
held us,
hid us.

Books warmed us
– we lived within
their covers.

My younger sister
sucked her thumb, banged her head
for years.

My elder sister
wore shorts with flies
to be a boy.

As if on a seesaw
I balanced between,
ate chocolate.

4

Imagine a house to fit the family:
study at the center, mother sitting
sometimes sewing by father's side,
large kitchen complex on the edge,
not yet easy with modern machines,
polished dining room, enormous lounge
 – saturated with students on Sundays –
 plenty of bedrooms, corners to creep into,
 attics and gardens for play and escape.

Ruth Hanchett

Perpetual pace

a friend once told me over tea
how the word wicked
gradually
over time was changing
in terms of
meaning and connotation

I replied - no hesitation –
how the word wicked
timelessly
to me would be the key
synonym
for this pulse within my skin

Cecile Bol

Boy (some advice)

once there will be an offbeat boy
just when you least expect it, not
notably handsome at first glance
but made attractive by his mind

a surprising thought, you could love
despite his ridiculous hair
not to mention his lack of style
details you could grow to foster

hip-hip-hurrah – for the first time
enticed by the soul not the skin
girl, you have become a woman
enjoy the notion while you can

'OMG, he's sooo fucking hot!'
facepalm – never read the comments...
gazillions hail his hair and style
'I'd blow him for his gorgeous cum!'

you'll swallow – vomit in your mouth
don't spit on your fresh victory
rule thirty-four a sure sniper
what is seen cannot be unseen

too late, what felt like a triumph
now nothing but failure – what boy
would want your impaired affection
while harems praise his perfection?

let go – let him become a man

maybe get married, have a child
just don't forget to remember
look back to secretly cherish

how once there was this offbeat boy
who broke your heart only to make
you see you know how to notice
what most never care to look for

Cecile Bol

father-daughter dance

I carry your surname
Like a dead weight
Yet there are no ghosts here.
The memories fresh
As the scars I wear
That I clean with each tear.
What poet am I
When words are yours
To use to trick my ear?
You repaint the past
Add in your crown
As I watch the crowd cheer.
And I am one of them
Believing each tale
Like you, it is the truth I fear.
So we stay stuck
In this father-daughter dance
Me left trailing at the rear.
You tell the world
Of daddy's little girl
While stealing each childhood year.
I played the part
And played it well
But I pray the end is near.

Jennifer Richards

Cradle to Grave

An end to the cradle for a grave little girl.
From teething to perfect white teeth she went.
From tottering feet to tottering, hell bent
in flimsy tops and arms aloft
laughing and singing until quietly spent.

An end to the pain for a growing young girl.
From gurgling to giggling she went.
From clinging hand to curling claw, hell bent
in fighting stance and drunken trance
bleeding and crying until quietly spent.

An end to the loss for this lost little girl.
From wriggling to writhing she went.
From smiling to smouldering, hell bent
on welcoming in and living easily with the sin,
whispering and teasing until quietly spent.

An end to the life of a tired little girl.
From this world to that she went.
From demons she ran hell bent
disarmed by fatherly charms then
choking and dreaming until quietly spent.

Richard Smith

A dead crab, white belly up

A dead crab, white belly up,
floating in the shallow pool, trapped among
low sandbanks, left behind under the
scorching sun when the waves retreated
Wind whispers ripples on the surface
moving the spindly legs as if they live

A dead girl, white belly up,
one hand floating in the pool
Wind whispers through her hair
moves the fingers in the water as
if they try to grab life

A child picks up the crab,
to bury it, he digs a hole in the sand
with his fingers
I took his spade to dig
a grave for the girl
We eye each other suspiciously
I suspect him of killing the crab

Nico Volkerts

The slight

Your fingers reach for a succulent summer peach
stars tingling deep in the tongue's chasm.

You could be Abraham raising the knife
and not sinning or an incongruous mongrel

trotting back, all birds alarmed into sky.
There are many ways to immaculate sanctuary.

Then there's a quixotic impulse, that
loose likeness you devised as a child, not you

now at home, living forwards understanding
backwards. Coats cling to the hall's coat stand.

His remark says there's poetry to be flagged down
impromptu as if stalled in the drift of a snowy forest

having left no clear note when setting out
of an intended route you still failed to follow,

it being quite useless to be left off guard
as if angry, uncaring or cleverly camouflaged.

Christopher James

The knack of flying

Nothing is linear.
Not the wavering decision
torn lustily, alarmingly from mouths
like a cavernous tooth
over the near-last cloudy soup
nor the stalked road out,
not the son sustaining the father's memory
locked like a roadblock in time
in hoisted manliness at fourteen
nor the intrigue of secret
in promiscuous cellars.

The decent future
will have none of the past's accumulations
ballast only and too heavy, bar
the family photos stitched into lining
and dollars for the stars. Backs against walls
and the walls in pieces and the pieces
jaggedly piled like an immense jigsaw
with no Sunday recreation.
They're flouting the intactness of time
it being known well before
this will be the gravest memory after.

They're filmed waiting, wiping noses
burying hands in pockets. Waiting –
some would have us see – like cats
that freeze when the bird turns:
the escape has all of the prison though.
And the bird flies. Freedom's
released to shit-houses, drying

by body heat. And with no exception
every table convulses like re-entry from space
when the man behind it
asks to see a document.

Christopher James

Art Appreciation

A tall sticklike figure with close-cropped hair
Back jeans and a light cotton T-shirt,
Unpainted, the only clue to her gender
The two little pimples that passed for her breasts.

She and a friend, a short buxom black girl
All lips and buttocks and in your face bling
Were discussing the various voluptuous forms
At the Henry More sculpture show.

"I don't get it," said Stick, "No one else I know
looks anything like any of these."
"no," shrugged the back girl, "too many holes
and them titchy heads, like they aint got no brains."

William Wood

Please Do Not Distract

As if the raw emotion and distress
Of Francis Bacon's cruel, bold paintings
Were not enough to digest and comprehend,
There came a blind man led by his dog
Through this close packed, puzzled throng
And twice the two completed a circuit
Of the ten rooms. A large yellow label
Attached to the placid hound's handle
Read, "I am working, please do not distract."

William Wood

Renaissance Room

In a room hung with classical portraits
Of virtuous, straight-backed beauties,
All blonde, cherry lipped and perfectly pale
A swarthy attendant sat slumped in her seat
Podgy and hot in her thick serge suit
Quite covered in security labels and badges
Like a clippie of yore on a London bus

William Wood

The Last Letter

July 27ᵗʰ 1890   imo Vincent van Gogh

My dear Theo,

In my life I brandished a blade;
A knife, full of yellow, bright as the midday sun,
To strike through the heart of my darkness.
And, as my colours burned and blazed,
The nightmares began to fade;
But oh, dear brother,
The storm clouds still gathered and waited.

I carried the tools of my trade and a loaded gun,
As the shadows of Saint Remy still stalked me.
I entered a field of windblown wheat,
Scattering the screeching crows with my first shot;
And I fixed them against field and sky,
As totems in ivory black;
Each one a memory of my madness.

And with a brush full of scarlet lake,
I drew a pathway, bright blood red, but a fugitive red;
I fear it will bleed from my canvas,
After my lifeblood has fled.

I write this now from my attic room;
Wounded, weary and alone.
I have slept, and I dreamed deeply;
And you were there Theo, head bowed,
Mourning by my bed.
And dear brother, I must also tell you this:

66

Beneath a clear blue, eternal sky,
I stood in a field of golden wheat;
Rich, ripe and ready for harvest.
The crows had vanished from my sight;
and though my brush had fallen now,
My work lived on.

And oh, dear brother:
I saw my paintings on museum walls;
and I heard a voice from the future call,
Amongst a sea of expectant faces.
And I saw his gavel about to fall;
And there Theo, there, carefully held in white gloved hands,
Was my portrait of Doctor Gachet...

Harvey Martin

Flash Fiction

Horseplay

Rumps bump on Chippendale legs. The horizon is a line of sweat and figures from Cervantes. Everything gives way to the horses' struggle – trees and sky are Indian paper. I forget for a moment that it's my fault. I threw the apples, thinking I was doing good, but the horses knew better. My wife is a trembling line in the distance but the horses fight on without us. I have thrown away something more than apples and the Spanish horses have read their Lorca.

Jonathan Page

Clashing colours

This time it was picking the paint for their window frames, much in need of repair, that lured them into a fight. He liked the warmth of mustard yellow. She was keen to insist on pale sea green. Or maybe a more neutral colour, in case they… if… They came home carrying two pots. Green on the moving parts, yellow on the rest would look great, so great indeed. A kiss, a hug, a smile, as they put their trust in their colourful compromise to keep out of sight, for another year or so, the rot extending underneath.

Cecile Bol

The First Time at her Place

The first time at her place. When I saw the Bunsen burner and tripod on the duvet I knew she liked to experiment in bed.

John Holland

Hatching Time V.1

Jeanie, a BTO Ornithologist, and I were in the Cullins, climbing to this eyrie I'd spotted. The pair of eagles soared above, watching.

We were photographing three eagle eggs plus one red egg as a hole appeared in the red one and a tiny winged lizard crawled out. Growing all the time it circled the nest seizing its own tail-end in its jaws and crushing the eggs.

Jeannie whispered, "The worm Ourouboros that swalloweth its tail..." The thing readied itself for flight as the eagles stooped and tore it to pieces "...but this one won't girdle the Earth."

Cedric Fox-Kirk

Kept Quiet

I wish Frank would speak to me – even his yelling makes me feel like me, you know? But he hasn't said anything since he told me off about the cutlery drawer. He was really angry; I was so scared I spilt some juice on the carpet, and…
Well. He hates the house being messy.
I scrubbed for hours. He usually loves watching me clean – all that bending over – but this time he just sat there, staring at the carpet as it slowly turned from red, to pink, to white again.
I've said I'm sorry.
But he won't listen.

Ben Howels

Alpha Male

Two days in, she knew he had to go.

Was it the endless gibbering over pre-dinner cocktails, the boasting about his back, sack and crack wax, green olives tossed into his gaping mouth?

No, it was the manicured finger laid pointedly on her forearm fluff.

"So unsightly, darling."

Anchored off an uninhabited island, she spots a possible replacement, swinging between trees. The crew bribed with diamonds, the drugged hulk is rowed ashore. Exchanged.

Now her new companion lounges beside her sipping a banana daiquiri. Hairy and silent, just how she likes them. A proper alpha male.

Caroline Deacon

Flip

Make no mistake, this is not about the money. Win or lose, I'll stay in the game. Each flip of the card, a chance to pin that dealer down, gain the upper hand.

And when I'm walking home, so skint I can't even afford a bus ticket, I'll be mulling over lines to the wife, the boss, my father. Excuses, apologies even. None of them heartfelt, none of them even close to the truth.

Because nothing beats the tingle of fingertips, deep in my pockets, stroking at thumbs. The after-burn of an ace, flipped to nail the win.

Jacqueline Winn

Flat for Sale

A must see!

Living room: good size, sofa in the corner where she would rest her head in his lap, safe.

Kitchen: small, though big enough to dance close on a Sunday morning to the smell of frying bacon.

Bathroom with a power shower strong enough that she couldn't tell water from tears.

Large master bedroom where she stretched her fingers out across the bed and learnt that loneliness is open space.

Nearest tube: just 5 miles away, near enough that he did not look back when he left.

Cost: Too high. Always, too high.

Catherine Perrins

Attack!

I wielded my sword above my head and slashed each letter x in half, but the cube sign simply meant that each half regenerated threefold ready to attack again. I scythed the brackets in the middle, mistakenly unleashing a plethora of angry numbers who want to destroy me. In a moment of inspiration, I slipped under a square root sign to create an army of mini-me united together in slaying my mathematical foe.

'The test has finished. Put your pen down.'

The teacher collects my blank test paper. I wink at the golden ratio sign. She stabs him dead.

Lisa Donoghue

One-upmanship

One elongated word for this funeral: *boooring*. Even more boring than Grandmother's and hers was a teeny affair with two mourners: me and Mother. What kind of person has two mourners? A bitter battleaxe, that's what, and I'm supposed to take after her.

Today is Mother's funeral, furnished with many mourners and many stories of her habitual benevolence.

I yawn, cough, splutter, retch.

People turn. Through watering eyes I see the minister watching. And waiting. This funeral is not *boooring*, for it's about to feature a real-time presentation of a sermon-stopping death.

At least I've got loads of mourners.

Sharon Boyle

Bested

Great concert, great atmosphere, great company – the greatest: his girlfriend. Correction – ex-girlfriend.

At interval his rehearsed proposal flooded the big screen.

His face: eager, confident.

Hers: crumbling confusion.

During the crowd's expectant silence she fled.

The screen showed his face pucker before he collected enough pride to rise from his kneel and shiver out shrugs and pseudo grins for flashing phones.

Three weeks of organisation plus five minutes of fame (or infamy) turned into months of humiliation. He was recognised and pitied. Correction – he was recognised, pitied and laughed at.

For some attendees it had bested the main act.

Sharon Boyle

Superyacht

The small boats rotate on their anchors like distressed clocks. A superyacht has seized the bay. It hangs like guilt over the watercolours of the harbour, the toy restaurants in pastel colours. The island evacuates its seabirds and the trees that fringe that narrow beach seek safety in their own thick hair. But what is it to live like that, apart and out of scale, what do you miss? The yacht is a blind hull, its superstructure bared abs untouched by time. It vanishes in the night, as if it knew the limits of ownership.

Jonathan Page

Peek-a-boo

She sits on a park bench dappled with morning sun, gazes into her pram, softly sings a lullaby.

The baby had kept her up all night, red-faced, relentlessly crying, flailing his arms and legs, refusing her efforts to nurse and comfort.

She leans closer, covers her face with her hands, opens them up, smiling. Peek-a-boo!

This is the motherhood she had imagined. Walks in the park, lullabies, peek-a-boo.

Returning home, as she approaches her door she hears her baby inside, still crying in his cot.

She turns, pushes her pram back to the park and softly sings a lullaby.

Supie Dunbar

Violently Beautiful

The small pool swirled as water a shade darker than turquoise bubbled restlessly, eager to escape. Little by little, the pool swelled, forming a perfect dome. Slowly, slowly, and then all at once, water shot through the bubble's center. Spouts of water climbed up, competing in a race where the clouds were the finish line. Then the geyser collapsed back to earth, the pool empty. The water flowing across the ground now was calm, the way a volcano could pass as a mountain before it exploded. Steam billowed through the air, the only evidence the eruption had occurred.

Eirlys Chui

A New Parent

Bright yellow tabs were sticking out where I needed to sign. I looked at Becca, my one remaining friend from primary school, and at the daughter sleeping in the sling pressed to her chest, and picked up the pen.

'Thank you, Joyce,' she said. 'It's just a legality.'

I nodded scribbling my name. 'The worst case scenario will never happen anyway,' I said, offering us both reassurance.

But it did. And now Matilda is snoring lightly in a cot in my house instead of her mother's, her dark curls lying damp on her forehead.

Laura Besley

Flying Solo

I'd never feel alone again, that's what I thought. I had the tests, found a suitable match, went through the (sometimes painful) procedures and then there was life. Heart beating, organs growing, limbs moving.

People kept telling me I was 'Oh so brave!' I smiled, nodded, thinking that being a mother is 'Oh so natural!'

But only weeks after Eva was born, I started feeling significantly less brave. I was tired, oh so tired. I staggered through the days and spent nights rocking a screaming baby. I wanted to scream too.

I've never felt so alone.

Laura Besley

Hatching Time V.2

Jeanie, a BTO Ornithologist, and I were in the Cullins, climbing to this eyrie I'd spotted. The pair of eagles soared above, watching.

We were photographing three eagle eggs plus one red egg as a hole appeared in the red one and a tiny winged lizard crawled out. Growing all the time it circled the nest seizing its own tail-end in its jaws and crushing the eggs.

Jeannie whispered, "The worm Ourouboros that swalloweth its tail..."

The thing flew off northwards.

"Isn't it supposed to girdle the Earth?" I asked."

"Oh it will," she whispered, "it will."

Cedric Fox-Kirk

~ The End ~

More from *Earlyworks Press*

We at Earlyworks Press invite the winner and the shortlisted authors from each of our writing competitions to submit work for an anthology. We are proud of the standard, variety and entertainment value of the resulting collections. Here is a selection…

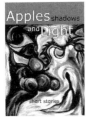

Apples, Shadows and Light
Where do baby selkies come from? Where do shadows go? What happens in the minutes after a war ends?
ISBN 978-1-910841-42-6 **£8.99**

Odds Against
A short story collection by competition short-listed author **Bruce Harris**
ISBN 9781910841443 **£8.99**

The Several Deaths of Finbar's Father
and other stories
ISBN 978-1-906451-96-7 **£8.99**

Don't look down! **Ways of Falling**
ISBN 978-1-906451-30-1, **£8.99**

Stories of Past, Present and Future
The Ball of the Future
Stories, long and short
ISBN 978-1-910841-25-9 **£8.99**

Flying colours, flowing colours, falling walls and courting pigeons: **sharp as lemons**
Poetry and Flash Fiction
ISBN 978-1-906451-95-0 **£7.99**

There is **at least £100 prize money** for first place in the competitions, always a free copy of the anthology and discounts on other books for authors – email **services@earlyworkspress.co.uk** for details, as well as the option of a discounted membership of the **Earlyworks Press Writers' Club**. If you would like to see your work featured in an Earlyworks Press anthology or would like more information about our publishing and book event activities, or to order books, please visit the website, where you can **sign up for our newsletter** on the Competitions Page, or follow **Earlyworks Press** on Facebook, or visit the editor's blog, **kaygreen.blog** on wordpress

www.earlyworkspress.co.uk